IRAN

Rourke Publishing

COUNTRIES IN CRISIS

DALE ANDERSON

www.rourkepublishing.com

PHOTO CREDITS: AFP/Getty Images: p. 36; Bettmann/Corbis: pp. 22, 23, 24; Vera Bogaerts/istock: p. 33;
Darren Booy/istock: p.19; Maj. Alayne Conway/U.S. Department of Defense: p. 42; Corbis: p. 18; Michael
Coyne/National Georgraphic/Getty Images: p. 29; Robert Ellis/istock: p. 35; Henghameh Fahimi/AFP/Getty
Images: pp. 30-31; The Gallery Collection/Corbis: p. 20; Graeme Gilmour/istock: p. 12; Javarman3/istock: pp.
14, 16; Alan Keler/Sygma/Corbis: p. 27; ATTA KENARE/AFP/Getty Images: p. 32; Klass Lingbeek-van
Kranen/istock: p. 15; Chris McGrath/Getty Images: p. 42; Behrouz Mehri/AFP/Getty Images: p. 40; Mark
Meyer/Time Life/Getty Images: p. 28; Valery Shanin/istock: p. 13; STF/AFP/Getty Images: p. 38; U.S. Coast
Guard: p. 5; Kontos Yannis/Corbis Sygma: p. 7; Daniella Zalcman/Wikimedia Commons: p. 8.

Cover picture shows women in burkas attending a ceremony to mark the 14th anniversary of the death of
Ayatollah Khomeini—the first Leader of the Revolution. [Javad Montazeri /Majority World/Still Pictures]

Produced for Rourke Publishing by Discovery Books
Editor: Gill Humphrey
Designer: Keith Williams
Map: Stefan Chabluk
Photo researcher: Rachel Tisdale

Library of Congress Cataloging-in-Publication Data

Anderson, Dale, 1953-
  Iran / Dale Anderson.
      p. cm. -- (Countries in crisis)
  Includes index.
  ISBN 978-1-60472-350-2
  1. Iran--Juvenile literature. I. Title.
  DS254.75.A53 2008
  955--dc22

                              2008016350

Printed in the USA

CONTENTS

CHAPTER ONE

A WAR OF WORDS

In January of 2002, President George W. Bush spoke to the U.S. Congress. In his speech he said some nations were part of an "axis of evil." These nations, he said, threatened world peace by helping terrorists. One of the nations he named was Iran. Why did President Bush say these things?

On September 11, 2001, terrorists attacked the United States. They hijacked passenger jets and flew them into buildings. Two planes destroyed the World Trade Center in New York City, killing more than 2,000 people. Another plane damaged the Pentagon, near Washington, D.C.

President Bush quickly vowed to fight against the terrorists who staged these attacks. He promised to punish any nation that helped terrorists. Soon after, Bush launched an attack on Afghanistan. He wanted to get rid of the Taliban government there because it had helped the September 11 terrorists. Iran, which had opposed the Taliban, supported the U.S. action. Since 1979 relations between Iran and the United States had been bitter. Now they seemed to be improving.

The ruins of the collapsed World Trade Center buildings still smoldering two weeks after the September 11, 2001, terrorist attacks. The attacks led the United States to launch a war on terrorism.

> " We were all shocked by the fact that the U.S. had such a short memory and was so ungrateful about what had happened just a month ago. "
>
> *Javad Zarif, Iranian government official, remembering (in 2006) the reaction to Bush's speech.*

THE PRESIDENT'S REASONS

President Bush had two main concerns. Firstly, the U.S. Central **Intelligence** Agency (CIA) had recently issued a warning about Iran. The nation, it said, was actively seeking to build nuclear weapons. The United States was worried about Iran having such powerful weapons.

The second reason was that Iran gave money and weapons to a group called Hezbollah. This organization, based in Lebanon, wanted to destroy Israel.

Israel is a close ally of the United States.

IRAN ANSWERS

Since that 2002 speech, Iranian and U.S. leaders have exchanged sharp words many times. The United States has been joined by countries around the world in calling on Iran to give up its nuclear program.

Fighters from the group Hezbollah celebrating after Israel withdrew its troops from Lebanon in 2000.

HEZBOLLAH

Hezbollah comes from Arabic words meaning *the Party of God*. The group was formed in 1979 and is funded by Iran. It aimed to push Israeli troops out of Lebanon. It also wanted to end Western influences in Lebanon and form an **Islamic** government there. The United States and other countries call it a terrorist group.

Iranian president Mahmoud Ahmadinejad has spoken harsh words against Israel and the United States. Here he speaks at Columbia University, in New York City, in 2007. The visit led to many protests against him.

DEFENDING IRAN

> I fought in the war between Iran and Iraq in the 1980s. . . .I lost some of the best years of my life fighting a war. But the war had no good result and that makes me really sad. . . .If they attack Iran, of course I will fight. But I will be fighting to defend Iran. . . my land. I will not be fighting for the government and the nuclear cause.
>
> *Hamid, interviewed by the BBC, April 28, 2006.*

These nations have blocked trade with Iran to pressure it to act.

Iran's leaders have protested. They are simply trying to develop nuclear energy, they say, not build weapons. In 2007, President Mahmoud Ahmadinejad of Iran called the United States a "bullying power." He also accused it of violating people's human rights.

Some Iranians fear that these harsh words might lead to war. At the same time, many Iranians are angry with their government for not doing more to improve the poor economy. Others want to see greater political freedom in Iran. Still, most Iranians don't like other countries telling Iran what to do.

CHAPTER TWO

A RICH HERITAGE

Iran is in Southwest Asia. It sits on the northern shores of the Persian Gulf and stretches north to the Caspian Sea. Turkey and Iraq border Iran on the west. Afghanistan and Pakistan border it on the east.

A large country, Iran has nearly 636,000 square miles (1.65 million sq. km). Mountains tower over the northwest and southwest. A high **plateau** rises in most of central Iran, with lowlands along the coast of the Persian Gulf. Two large deserts cover much of the eastern part of the country.

Rocky soil and little rain make much of Iran hard to farm. The land has other riches, though. Iran has the third largest oil deposits in the world and the second largest natural gas reserves. These fuels can be burned to power cars and trucks, heat homes, and make electricity. Selling oil and gas is an important source of income to Iran.

More than 71 million people live in Iran. Two-thirds of them live in cities. The great majority of Iranians are Persians. Almost all of Iran's people are **Muslims**.

Iran has an ancient history that stretches back thousands of years. For most of that history, it was known as Persia.

BUILDING AN EMPIRE

The first people known to live in Iran settled there about 100,000 years ago. Small kingdoms arose

WHERE IS IRAN?

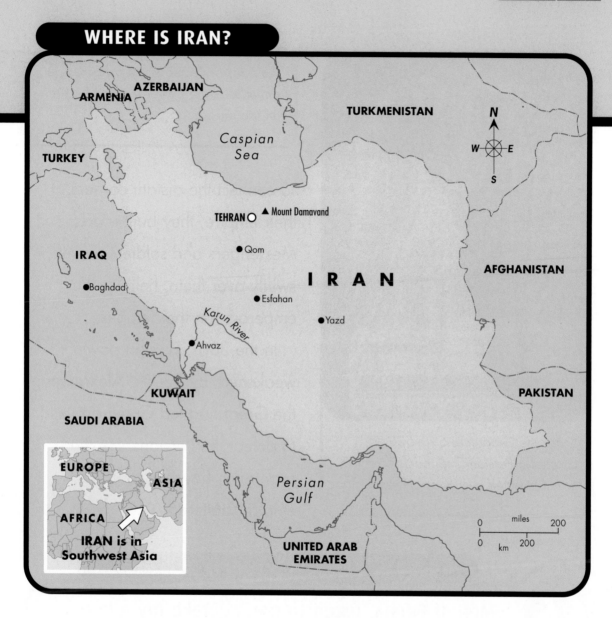

ARMENIA
AZERBAIJAN
TURKMENISTAN

Caspian Sea

TURKEY

TEHRAN ○   ▲ Mount Damavand

IRAQ

AFGHANISTAN

● Qom

I R A N

● Baghdad

● Esfahan

Karun River

● Yazd

● Ahvaz

KUWAIT

PAKISTAN

SAUDI ARABIA

EUROPE

ASIA

AFRICA

IRAN is in
Southwest Asia

Persian
Gulf

UNITED ARAB
EMIRATES

miles
0   200
0   200
km

in the area and competed with each other for power. Then, around 550 BC, Cyrus the Great defeated the kingdom of the Medes to form the Persian **Empire**. He and his successors conquered other lands, reaching as far as Egypt. Cyrus's empire lasted about two hundred years. The Persian emperors sat in their impressive capital cities and received taxes from the conquered peoples.

Cyrus the Great (ca. 590–529 BC) created a Persian Empire in ancient Iran that lasted over two hundred years.

The ruins of Persepolis stand as a reminder of the power that the Persian Empire once had.

To connect the distant corners of their empire, they built roads. Messengers and soldiers moved swiftly over them, helping the emperors run their empire.

In the 300s, Persian power weakened. By 330 BC Alexander the Great had led Greek armies to defeat the Persians. He died soon after, however, and his empire shattered.

CYRUS'S WORDS?INSPIRE THE PERSIANS

" Men of Persia, listen to me. . . .Take my advice and win your freedom. I am the man destined to undertake your liberation, and it is my belief that you are a match for the Medes in war as in everything else.

Reported by the Greek historian Herodotus (ca. 484–425 BC).

TWO NEW EMPIRES

About 250 BC, a people called the Parthians came to control Persia. They ruled the area for nearly five hundred years. During this time, they fought several wars with the Romans. Though Roman armies were very powerful, they could never defeat the Parthians.

The Parthian Empire finally weakened. By AD 230, a king named Ardashir had defeated the Parthian armies and ruled Persia. He was descended from a king named Sasan. For that reason, his **dynasty** is called the Sasanian dynasty.

ZOROASTRIANISM

A new religion arose in Persia around 600 BC. It was called Zoroastrianism, after the prophet who founded it. Zoroaster broke with many religions of the ancient world. He said there was just one god, not many. Persian rulers followed the religion. They claimed that this god, named Ahura Mazda, helped them rule.

The city of Yazd, in central Iran, is now home to the largest group of followers of Zoroastrianism in Iran. Many Zoroastrians fled to this city in the seventh century AD, when Muslim Arabs conquered Iran.

Modern buildings in Tehran rise against the dramatic Elburz Mountains. Dating from the fourth century AD, Tehran has been the capital of Iran since the 1780s.

Sasanian rulers led Persia for about 400 years. During this time, rulers took the title shahanshah. This word means *king of kings* and is often shortened to shah. The Sasanians ruled what is now western India to modern Iraq.

CHAPTER THREE

A MUSLIM LAND

In the early 600s, a new power arose in Southwest Asia. It was the religion of Islam, and it changed the region, and the world.

Islam started in the Arabian **peninsula** in the 600s. The prophet Muhammad preached that people had to follow the only god, Allah. His followers spread the religion to new lands. By 642, they had conquered Persia. By 732, Muslim armies had spread from modern Pakistan all the way across North Africa.

The Imam Mosque in Esfahan is one of the glories of Iran. Built in the 1600s, the building is decorated with tiny tiles in seven colors that are assembled in complex patterns like those on the dome.

SHIITES AND SUNNIS

Not all Muslims are Shiites. Some are Sunnis. Sunnis believe that the caliph who followed Ali had a right to rule. Sunnis are the majority in most Muslim countries, though not in Iran. Tension between Shiites and Sunnis has caused problems in the Muslim world since the 600s.

At first, all these lands were unified under one ruler, the **caliph**. He was not only a political ruler but also a religious leader. This vast empire was difficult to control. Persians often revolted against foreign leaders. Now these revolts also had a religious basis. In 656, Ali, Muhammad's cousin and son-in-law, became caliph. Those opposing his rule killed Ali and seized the throne. Some Muslims never accepted the caliphs who came after Ali. They believed that Ali and his successors should lead Islam. They came to be called the Shi'at Ali, or *followers of Ali*. Today, they are called Shiites. Most Persians were Shiites.

PERSIAN RULERS AND WRITERS

Between 821 and 1055, some leaders in Persia gained control of some parts of the area. Though they saw the caliph as the overall leader, they ran their areas themselves.

Under these rulers, Persian literature flourished. At the beginning of the eleventh century, a Persian writer named Ferdawsi wrote a long poem called the Shah-nameh, or *Book of Kings*.

This battle scene decorates a copy of Ferdawsi's Shah-nameh. Artists of Persia became famous for their colorful, elaborate paintings that illustrated books.

A mix of history and legend, the poem is still loved in Iran today. In the 1100s, Omar Khayyam wrote beautiful short poems. In the 1200s, Jalal ad-Din Rumi wrote poems that explored the relationship between humans and Allah.

FOREIGN RULE

In the early 1200s, Mongol fighters overran Persia. In 1256, they killed the last caliph and took power. The Mongols ruled for only a hundred years, but they changed life in Iran forever.

Tradition says that people first moved into the caves of Kandovan, in northern Iran, to escape the invading Mongols. Some people still use the caves as homes.

THE COMING OF THE MONGOLS

" One division. . .passed on into [Persia], until they had made an end of taking possession, and destroying, and slaying [killing], and plundering [robbing], and thence passing on to [other parts of Persia], and the cities contained therein,. . .destroying [the cities] and slaying most of their inhabitants.

Iban al-Athir, writing about the Mongol conquest of Persia (1220–1221). "

SHAH ABBAS (1571–1629)

Greatest of the Safavid rulers was Shah Abbas. He defeated several enemies to expand the empire's territories. The shah also gained a reputation for being just and fair. During his rule, Persian craft workers became famous for weaving beautiful carpets.

THE SAFAVID EMPIRE

In 1501, a Persian leader named Ismail gained control of Persia. He began a new dynasty called the Safavids. Following tradition, Ismail took the title of shah. He claimed that his family was descended from Ali. The Safavids ruled Persia for more than 200 years. There was a period of prosperity at the beginning of their rule and also some great artistic achievements. The new capital of Persia, Esfahan, became renowned for its beauty.

The Safavids weakened and lost power in 1736. For nearly two hundred years, weak shahs ruled the land. After the discovery of oil, Britain and Russia competed for control and influence in Persia. During World War I Persia was occupied by British and Russian troops. The British pulled out in 1918.

This painting of a royal hunt from the 1600s shows the richness of the Safavid period. Note that some of the hunters ride elephants.

THE CREATION OF IRAN

A new leader, named Reza Khan, emerged in the 1920s. In 1925 he ousted the shah and took the throne himself. He changed his name to Reza Shah Pahlavi.

In 1935, Reza Shah changed the country's name to Iran. New laws changed the face of Iran. Many matters were taken away from the Islamic courts, that were run by clerics, or religious leaders. These courts traditionally followed Islamic law. The new courts were put under the control of the government, and the judges were government officials. New laws banned the veils (face coverings) that women traditionally had worn. Still, people enjoyed very few political freedoms.

When World War II broke out, Reza Shah's friendship with Germany made Iran an enemy of the British and Russians. They invaded Iran and forced the shah to give up the throne. In 1941 they put his son, Mohammed Reza, in his place.

Reza Shah Pahlavi named his country Iran and worked to modernize it after taking power in the 1920s.

During World War II, Reza Shah allied himself with Germany. The British, shown here, and the Soviet Union (a group of communist republics led by Russia) sent troops to Iran to take control. They didn't want Iran's oil going to Germany.

CHAPTER FOUR

THE ISLAMIC REVOLUTION

Iran prospered from its oil wealth. The country first began pumping oil from its vast reserves in the 1920s. Selling oil to other countries became an important source of income to the country under Shah Mohammad Reza. The shah's government also gave poor

Shah Mohammad Reza sits on the Peacock Throne, flanked by his wife and son. The original Peacock Throne had been stolen from India by a Safavid ruler in the 1700s. It was later lost, and a replica was built and used by several rulers of Iran.

AYATOLLAH KHOMEINI (1902–1989)

Ruhollah Khomeini was both the son and grandson of Muslim religious teachers. He became famous in Iran for his understanding of Islamic law, and for his criticism of the shah's policies. In the 1950s, he was given the honorary title of **ayatollah**, a tribute to his reputation as a holy man. After Khomeini's death, Ayatollah Ali Khamenei was appointed Leader for life.

farmers a chance to own the land they worked. A middle class grew, and many Iranians enjoyed comfortable lives. Other reforms improved health care.

Iranians welcomed many of these changes. At the same time, the shah's rule was harsh. His secret police had the power to arrest anyone and hold them as long as they wished. People feared speaking out.

Still, some people did protest. Many of these were Islamic clerics, or religious leaders. Islam had a deep hold on many Iranians. Some more conservative people resented the way the country was becoming modernized. They felt it was moving away from Islam. The clerics agreed, complaining that the new laws violated the teachings of Islam. Some Iranians supported the clerics' views because they opposed the shah. One of those critics was Ruhollah Khomeini. The government forced him into **exile** in 1964.

THE RISE OF THE AYATOLLAH

Though exiled, Khomeini remained influential. He sent speeches and writings back to his followers in Iran. As opposition to the shah grew stronger, Khomeini's words fueled the unrest. Worried about his safety, the shah fled the country in January 1979.

On February 1, Khomeini returned to Iran and was met by huge cheering crowds. Two months later, Iran's people voted to declare Iran an Islamic republic.

ISLAMIC RULE

In the new government, laws had to follow the teachings of Islam. While a president ran the government, he was not the top leader. That was the Leader of the Revolution, a religious leader. The first Leader was Khomeini. The Leader has great power. He names the commanders of the nation's armed forces and other officials. He can declare war and peace and set policies.

CALL FOR REVOLUTION

66 It is the duty of Islamic scholars and all Muslims to put an end to this system of oppression and, for the sake of the well-being of hundreds of millions of human beings, to overthrow these oppressive governments and form an Islamic government.

Ayatollah Khomeini, speaking from exile, 1970. 99

On his return to Iran in 1979, Ayatollah Khomeini was greeted by adoring crowds like this one at Tehran University.

The new Islamic law undid many of the changes made by the shah. Again, crimes were punished as the **Qu'ran** ordered. Women, who had begun to enjoy more freedoms, were told to cover their faces.

IRAN AND THE UNITED STATES

Khomeini called the United States *the Great Satan*. One reason for his dislike was because the U.S. had supported the shah for many years. Also, Khomeini was angered by the growing influence of Western culture on Muslims.

WELCOME BACK TO FREEDOM

After being held for more than a year, 53 American hostages were finally released by Iran in January 1981. Here some of the hostages leave the plane that carried them to freedom.

Late in 1979, President Jimmy Carter agreed to let the former shah come to the United States for medical care. Outraged college students stormed the American **embassy** in Tehran. They quickly seized dozens of Americans as **hostages**.

Iranian soldiers pray during a break in fighting in the Iran-Iraq War. Memory of the war still scars many Iranians.

While they were held, President Jimmy Carter cut off **diplomatic** relations with Iran. He froze all Iranian money held in U.S. banks. The hostages, more than 50 of them, were finally released in January 1981, but relations between Iran and the United States remained poor.

WAR WITH IRAQ

Iran and Iraq had long been rivals for power in Southwest Asia. In 1980, Iraq invaded Iran. The Iraqi army had some success at first, but the Iranians fought back. Iran's army regained the land that had been lost.

By 1982, though, the war had become a stalemate. Neither side could gain an advantage. This costly war finally ended in 1988. By then, about 200,000 Iranians had lost their lives.

CHAPTER FIVE

THE CRISIS AT HOME

The war caused great suffering and hardship. The country's economy stalled. Damage to oil facilities cut the amount of oil that Iran could produce and sell. This reduced the amount of money the government had to rebuild cities and provide jobs. Hundreds of thousands of Iranians had two or three jobs to make ends meet.

Another problem was a rapidly growing population. In the first 17 years after the revolution, Iran's population doubled. That put a strain on housing, the job market, and schools. During the middle 1990s, people took to the streets to protest the lack of jobs and opportunities. Some demonstrations turned violent.

Adding to the problems was a power grab by clerics. In 1996 elections for the legislature were held.

Tens of thousands of Iranians live in poverty because of a struggling economy.

Religious leaders ruled that nearly half of the candidates could not run. Many of these candidates had wanted more moderate policies than the clerics would accept. Meantime, the clerics shut down many newspapers for criticizing the government.

REFORMERS IN POWER

In 1997, Iranians elected Mohammad Khatami as their new president. Khatami was a moderate who wanted to create more freedom and take away some of the limits on women's rights. Newspapers enjoyed freedom to publish their views. Reformers won victories in local

Mohammad Khatami became president of Iran because the majority of Iranians wanted to see reforms and an end to the conservative policies of the clerics.

UNREST AMONG WOMEN

> " I have read about democracy, freedom of religion and freedom of expression in other countries and would like us to have the same in Iran. . .Equality of men and women does not exist in Iran. "
>
> *Maheen, a 60-year-old woman, in a BBC interview in 2006.*

elections in 1999, and Khatami was reelected in 2001.

Still, the reformers could not put all their plans into action. The structure of the government allowed conservative clerics to block many reforms. The failure of the reformers to achieve real change led to much discontent among the people. In 2003, 94 percent of Iranians said that the country desperately needed reform. Nearly three-quarters said that they thought the country needed to change its form of government.

Two women walk near a mosque at the holy city of Qom. The women have covered nearly all their bodies, as required by Iranian law. Some women challenge the law by not covering their heads, but they risk arrest for this offense.

MAHMOUD AHMADINEJAD (1956–)

A university student in the late 1970s, Ahmadinejad helped stage demonstrations against the shah. After the Islamic revolution, he earned his degree and fought in the Iran-Iraq War. He became mayor of Tehran in 2003. Two years later, he was elected president. He is controversial in other countries for his hostile statements about Israel and other matters.

A SURPRISING NEW LEADER

The reform movement angered religious leaders. In the 2004 parliamentary elections, they once again blocked large numbers of candidates who were pushing for reforms. The next year, they used their influence to help a little-known candidate, Mahmoud Ahmadinejad, win the presidential election.

Once in office, Ahmadinejad became very active. He fired thousands of government workers.

He put new economic policies in place. Opposition grew, however. Members of Ahmadinejad's own political party objected to some of his policies. Fifty economists wrote an open letter saying that his economic policies were a disaster.

IRAN IN 2008

By 2006, Iran's economy had begun to improve. Rising oil prices had given the government large amounts of cash. Still, trade with other countries was slow. As a

An offshore drilling platform in the sea off the coast of Iran. Many Iranians are angry that the government has not used its oil wealth to build a stronger economy.

result, the Iranian people suffered. By 2007, 40 percent of Iran's people lived in poverty. Fifteen percent of all workers were without jobs, and prices were rising fast.

In addition to the country's many economic problems, there was another concern.

Students marching at Tehran University protest an appearance there by President Ahmadinejad. The president faces growing unrest at home.

HARD TIMES IN IRAN

> In dozens of interviews in Tehran and other cities last year, Iranians from all walks of life. . .[said that] the government. . .has fallen short. It is hard to find a good job, difficult to pay the bills and, for a population where the [average] age is just a shade under 25, the future seems bleak.
>
> *Christine Spolar, reporting in the* Chicago Tribune, *January 23, 2007.*

Iran's best educated citizens were leaving the country in huge numbers. Each year up to 150,000 young people with college degrees left Iran for another country. These highly trained workers were no longer available to help build a better future for Iran.

Economic troubles were causing growing unrest in Iran. In elections held in 2006, voters chose many candidates who opposed Ahmadinejad's policies. President Ahmadinejad's term of office is set to expire in 2009. With little support at home, he looks unlikely to win the election. Meanwhile, though, Iran faced another crisis, this time in its relations with other countries.

CHAPTER SIX

THE CRISIS ABROAD

The Islamic Republic of Iran has had rocky relations with other countries. From the start, leaders of other Muslim nations in the region worried that Iran would spread its Islamic revolution to their countries. These leaders often worked together to oppose growing Iranian power in the region. During the Iran-Iraq War, many of these leaders supported Iraq, even though they disliked its leader. They hoped that the war would weaken Iran.

Women mourn the deaths of family members in the tragic accident of 1988. A wall painting depicts the cause of the accident, which happened when a U.S. navy ship accidentally shot down an Iranian passenger plane.

NOT TALKING

"
It's been 27 years since we've had a normal diplomatic, social, and political relationship [between Iran and the United States]. And so. . . I am one of the people responsible for Iran in our government and yet I have never met an Iranian government official in my 25-year career.

Nicholas Burns, U.S. diplomat, to a BBC reporter in 2006.

"

Ever since the hostage crisis of 1979, Iran and the United States have had poor relations. During the 1980s and 1990s, the United States banned much of its trade with Iran. In addition, several new incidents caused tension between the two countries. In 1988, a U.S. navy ship accidentally shot down an Iranian passenger plane. Nearly 300 people on board died. In 1993, Iran's leaders criticized the United States for interfering in Southwest Asia. Iran's support of Hezbollah and other groups became a growing source of tension, too. In 1995, President Bill Clinton further cut trade with Iran for this reason.

THE NUCLEAR ISSUE

The nuclear issue arose as a major problem after 2001. Iran's leaders said that they only wanted to develop nuclear energy.

American officials claimed they were trying to make **nuclear weapons**.

In 2003, the International Atomic Energy Agency (IAEA), part of the **United Nations (UN)** stepped in. It sent inspectors to Iran to look at the work being done there. The IAEA said Iran had not fully reported its activities. That increased concerns among world leaders that Iran was trying to hide something.

For the next four years, the United States and other nations pushed Iran to halt this work. Iran refused. In 2006, the United States convinced the United Nations Security Council to halt trade with Iran because of its nuclear program.

A NEW IRAQ WAR

While these disputes were going on, another problem arose. In 2003, the United States invaded Iraq to overthrow its leader, Saddam Hussein. Almost immediately rebels began to fight the new government with bomb attacks and shootings. American officials said that Iran gave money and weapons to some of these rebels. Officials from the two countries continued to argue on this issue.

A worker watches the control panel of a nuclear facility in Iran. Iran's leaders say that their nuclear research is only aimed at developing energy.

NEW TURNS

Late in 2007, U.S. intelligence agencies said that Iran had stopped trying to make nuclear weapons. President Bush said that Iran was still dangerous, but he couldn't convince other countries to follow his call for more tough sanctions.

Meanwhile, Iran declared that, in future, it would not talk with the United States and its allies on the nuclear issue. It would only deal with the IAEA.

Leaders of other countries in Southwest Asia also remained worried about Iran's power. In January 2008, President Bush echoed these concerns. "Iran's actions threaten the security of nations everywhere," he said. Iran's foreign minister dismissed the president's charges.

With American soldiers looking on, Iraqis clear the rubble after the explosion of car bombs in Baghdad. American leaders accuse Iran of giving money and weapons to support the rebels fighting the Iraqi government, and killing U.S troops there.

Thousands protested the visit of President Ahmadinejad to the United States in 2007. Some of the signs criticize the Iranian president for his doubts about the Holocaust. The Holocaust was the killing of more than 6 million Jews by Adolf Hitler's Nazi German government during World War II.

Even if Iran was not making nuclear weapons, its relations with other countries remained strained.

NOT GIVING IN

" Americans are mistaken by thinking that by pressuring Iran over the nuclear issue they can break Iran. By bringing this and other issues to the fore, they cannot bring the Iranian nation to its knees.

Ayatollah Khamenei, quoted on Iranian state television, January 13, 2008.

TIMELINE

BC

1000 First Persians enter Iran.

ca. 600 Zoroaster forms Zoroastrianism.

550 Cyrus the Great forms Persian Empire.

330 Alexander the Great conquers Persian Empire.

250 Parthian Empire begins; lasts until AD 230.

AD

230 Sasanian dynasty begins.

642 Muslim Arabs conquer Persia.

661 Ali killed; his followers become Shiites.

821 Regional leaders start controlling parts of Persia.

1220 The Mongols begin conquest of Persia.

1501 Safavid Empire begins.

1736 Safavid Empire loses power.

1925 Reza Khan becomes shah.

1935 Persia's name is changed to Iran.

1941 CIA-aided coup ousts Reza Khan, puts Mohammed Reza Pahlavi in power.

1964 Ayatollah Khomeini forced into exile; continues to criticize shah.

1979 Shah of Iran flees; Ayatollah Khomeini returns; Islamic Republic of Iran formed.

1979-1981 U.S. hostage crisis

1980-1988 Iran-Iraq War

1989 Ayatollah Khomeini dies; Ayatollah Khameini becomes Leader of the Revolution.

1995 U.S. President Bill Clinton imposes sanctions on Iran.

1997 Khatami elected to first of two terms as president; he promises reforms, but his efforts are blocked by religious leaders.

1999 Reform-minded candidates win elections to legislature.

2001 U.S. accuses Iran of seeking to build nuclear weapons.

2002 U.S. President George Bush calls Iran part of "axis of evil".

2003 IAEA conducts first inspections of Iranian nuclear sites; Iran agrees to slow nuclear research.

2005 Mahmoud Ahmadinejad wins election as Iran's president.

2006 UN Security Council approves sanctions against Iran for its nuclear research.

2007 U.S. intelligence says Iran stopped weapons research years before.

2008 U.S. President Bush calls Iran a dangerous state.

FACT FILE

IRAN

GEOGRAPHY

Area: 636,000 square miles (1.65 million sq. km.)

Borders: Iraq, Turkey, Azerbaijan, Armenia, Turkmenistan, Afghanistan, Pakistan

Terrain: Mountains in northwest, southwest; central and eastern plateau

Highest point: Mt. Damavand, 18,934 ft. (5,771 m)

Resources: oil, natural gas

Major rivers: Safid Rud, Karun, Kharkeh

SOCIETY

Population (2007): 71.2 million plus about 720,000 refugees from Afghanistan and Iraq

Ethnic groups: Persian 51%; Azeri 24%; Gilaki and Mazandarani 8%; Kurdish 7%; Other 10%

Languages: Persian; Azeri Turkish; Kurdish; others

Literacy: 77%

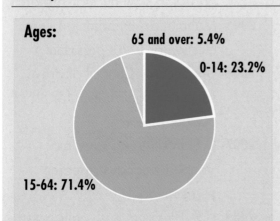

Ages:
- 65 and over: 5.4%
- 0-14: 23.2%
- 15-64: 71.4%

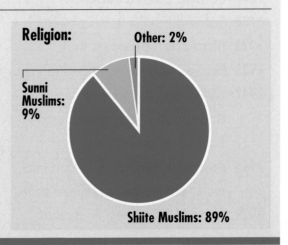

Religion:
- Other: 2%
- Sunni Muslims: 9%
- Shiite Muslims: 89%

GOVERNMENT

Type: Theocratic (religious) republic

Capital: Tehran   **Provinces**: 24

Independence: April 1, 1979 (Islamic Republic of Iran proclaimed)   **Law**: Based on Islamic law

Vote: Males and females 18 years

System: Chief of state: religious leader (chosen for life); head of government: president (elected every 4 years); legislature: Consultative Assembly (elected every 4 years)

ECONOMY

Currency: Iranian rial

Labor force (2006): 24.3 million

Total value of goods and services (2006): $599.2 billion

Poverty: 40% of the population below poverty line

Main industries: Petroleum, petrochemicals, fertilizers, textiles, cement

Foreign debt (2006): $141.4 billion

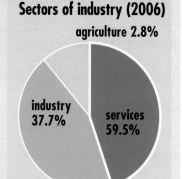

Sectors of industry (2006)

agriculture 2.8%

industry 37.7%

services 59.5%

COMMUNICATIONS AND MEDIA

Telephones (2006): 22.0 million fixed line; 12.7 million mobile

Internet users (2006): 18 million **TV stations:** 28 stations; Islamic Republic of Iran Broadcasting (IRIB) (state-run) **Newspapers:** 20 national dailies, including *Tehran Times* and *Iran Times* (both state-run)   **Radio:** AM 72; FM 5; shortwave 5; IRIB (state-run)

Airports: 129   **Railroads:** 5,817 miles (8,367 km)   **Roads:** 111,338 miles (179,288 km)

Ships: 131 over 1,000 tons   **Ports:** Assaluyeh, Bushehr

MILITARY

Branches: Army, navy, air force

Service: 18-month compulsory service for males when reaching age 18

GLOSSARY

ayatollah (EYE-uh-tole-uh): title for a major religious leader among Shiite Muslims

caliph (KAH-lef): religious and political leader of the united Muslim world

diplomatic (DIP-lo-mat-ic): good and tactful dealings with people generally, or with leaders of countries

dynasty (DIE-nuh-stee): a family that rules the same country or empire for many years

embassy (EM-buh-see): official office of one government in the territory of another country

empire (EM-pier): a kingdom that includes many lands and peoples

exile (ECKS-ile): being forced to live away from one's home country

hostage (HOSS-tuhj): someone being held in conditions like arrest for political reasons

intelligence (in-TELL-uh-jens): actions by members of a government aimed at learning the secret actions and plans of other countries

Islamic (i-SLAHM-ik): based on the religion and teachings of the Prophet Muhammad

legislature (LEJ-is-laychur): part of the government that passes laws

Muslims (MUHS-lims): people who follow the religion of Islam

nuclear weapons (NOO-klee-uhr WEP-ons): powerful weapons that can destroy entire cities

peninsula (puh-NIN-soo-lah): a piece of land with water on three sides

plateau (plah-TOO): flat land raised high above sea level

Qu'ran (kor-AN): the holy book of Islam

United Nations (UN) (yoo-NI-tid NAY-shuhns): the organization of countries set up after World War II to work for peace

FURTHER INFORMATION

WEBSITES

CIA Factbook: Iran

https://www.cia.gov/library/publications/
the-world-factbook/geos/ir.html
The site has facts and statistics on Iran.

BBC Middle East News

http://news.bbc.co.uk/1/hi/world/middle
_east/country_profiles/790877.stm
*This site offers the latest news, a timeline,
country profile, and links.*

Government of Iran

http://www.parstimes.com/gov_iran.html
*This site has lots of factual information
about Iran.*

Islamic Republic of Iran
News Agency

http://www.iran-daily.com/1386/
3040/html/
*This online news agency has up-to-date
information on recent events.*

Islamic History

http://www.uga.edu/islam/history.html
*This site has a lot of information
about Islamic history as well as timelines
and maps.*

BOOKS

Iran (Opposing Viewpoints). Laura K.
Egendorf, ed. Detroit, MI: Greenhaven
Press, 2005.

The Iranian Revolution. Brendan January.
Minneapolis, MN: Twenty-First Century
Books, 2007.

Iran in the News. Amy Graham. Berkeley
Heights, NJ: MyReportLinks.com, 2006.

Is Iran a Threat to Global Security?
Julia Bauder, ed. Detroit, MI: Greenhaven
Press, 2005.

INDEX